NAPOLEON QUOTES ON VICTORY, LEADERSHIP AND THE ART OF WAR

Selected and Edited by Mete Aksoy

CONTENTS

(According to Napoleon, in war the first principle of a commander is to conceal what he is doing.)

(According to Napoleon, in war men are nothing; one man is everything. The presence of a commander is indispensable. Also, according to Napoleon, a commander is the head, the whole of an army. An army is nothing without the head.)

INTRODUCTION

When the book was prepared, our example was Sun Tzu's "The Art of War" book. Like the timeless work of Sun Tzu, Napoleon's comments on the art of war were selected, edited and categorized. I have been working on leadership and art of war for nearly twenty years. I believe that the way to be able to fully understand what crosses great captains' minds is to examine the texts they write and the words they say.

However, the method I'm talking about here is not to try to solve the secrets of the mind by taking 20-30 quotations that a great captain says. I try to read everything that comes out of that leader's pen or mouth. So, how much secrets they hide and how much disinformation they do, after a long review, the patterns of the leaders among the things they write and say start to reveal themselves as secret codes. Of course, I do not stop there, I look at these patterns to see if that leader is practicing them in his life. If he does not, I discard the patterns that I find, but if the leader does, I try to deepen or analyze and finally synthesize that pattern.

Napoleon is one of the leaders I've read most in about twenty years. I have read most of the texts written by Napoleon and many of Napoleon's words, as well as reliable biographies about Napoleon. I have found some of the patterns that overlap Napoleon's words he had practiced in his life. By reviewing these 16 patterns in chapters, I have gathered Napoleon's comments in 16 chapters. The result is this book. Readers can trust that the comments and maxims really are Napoleon's because most of these comments are from the memories of the people who were with Napoleon until his last moments.

I used some comments/maxims in the in different chapters. Please do not be surprised. The reason why I used some comments/maxims a few times is that these comments belong to several chapters. For example, a quote/maxim belongs to both leadership and courage. In total, there are more than 300 different, original Napoleon comments/maxims in this book.

I believe that Napoleon's these thoughts and comments which I gathered and classified into 16 chapters, will lead commanders, businessmen/women, and individuals to victory when they face struggles.

M. Aksoy

VICTORY AND GLORY

(According to Napoleon, to live without victory and glory is to die every day.)

Death is nothing, but to live defeated and without glory is to die every day.

****

In giving battle a general should regard it as his first duty to maintain the honor and glory of his arms.

To spare his troops should be but a secondary consideration.

But the same determination and perseverance which promote the former object are the best means of securing the latter.

In a retreat you lose, in addition to the honor of your arms, more men than in two battles.

For this reason, you should never despair while there remain brave men around the colors.

This is the conduct which wins and deserves to win, the victory.

****

You do not get peace by shouting "Peace!"... Peace is a meaningless word; what we need is a glorious peace.

****

A good general, good officer, commissioned and non-commissioned, good organization, good instruction and strict discipline make good troops independently of the cause for which they are fighting.
But enthusiasm, love of country and the desire of contributing to the national glory may also animate young troops with advantage.

****

There is but one honorable way of being made a prisoner of war; that is by being taken separately and when you can no longer make use of your arms.
Then there are no conditions - for there can be none, consistently with honor - but you are compelled to surrender by absolute necessity.

****

An ordinary general occupying a bad position, if surprised by a superior force, seeks safety in retreat;

but a great captain displays the utmost determination and advances to meet the enemy.

By this movement he disconcerts his adversary;

and if the march of the latter evinces irresolution, an able general, profiting by the moment of indecision, may yet hope for victory or at least employ the day in maneuvering;

and at night he can entrench himself or fall back on a better position.

By this fearless conduct, he maintains the honor of his arms, which forms so essential a part of the strength of an army.

****

Nothing can excuse a general who avails himself of the knowledge he has acquired in the service of his country to give up its bulwarks to a foreign nation.

That is a crime abhorrent to the principles of religion, morality, and honor.

****

Praise from enemies is suspicious;

it cannot flatter an honorable man unless it is given after the cessation of hostilities.

****

Prisoners of war do not belong to the power for which they have fought;
they all are under the safeguard of honor and generosity of the nation that has disarmed them.
The military institutions of the English are faulty. They recruit only for money, although they often empty their prisons into their regiments. Their discipline is cruel.
With trifling considerations, small vanities, and petty passions, it is never possible to accomplish anything great.

****

One obtains everything from men by appealing to their sense of honor.

****

You must cite examples such as that of Marshal Mortier at Krems, and a great number of others that fill our annals, to demonstrate that in the past armed columns have found a way to break out by seeking all of their resources in their courage, that he who prefers death to ignominy saves himself and lives with honor, while on the contrary, the man who prefers life dies by covering himself with shame.

****

What I want you to preserve is the honor, and not a few planks and men.

****

I should like the disciplinary rules that are to be drawn up for the navy to give the officers no more right to beat our sailors than they have to beat our soldiers because it is an absolute principle of the French that every blow received must be returned.

****

Instead of the lash, I would lead them by the stimulus of honor. I would instill a degree of emulation into their minds. I would promote every deserving soldier, as I did in France...

****

What might not be expected of the English army if every soldier hoped to be made a general provided he showed the ability? (General) Bingham says, however, that most of your soldiers are brutes and must be driven by the stick. But surely the English soldiers must be possessed of sentiments sufficient to put

NAPOLEON QUOTES ON VICTORY, LEADERSHIP AND THE ART OF WAR

them at least upon a level with the soldiers of other countries, where the degrading system of the lash is not used. Whatever debases man cannot be serviceable.

****

Soldiers! You are ill-fed and almost naked. The government owes you a great deal, but it can do nothing for you. Your patience and courage do you honor but give you neither worldly goods nor glory. I shall lead you into the most fertile plains on earth. There you shall find great cities and rich provinces. There you shall find honor, glory, riches. Soldiers of the Army of Italy! Could encourage and constancy possibly fail you?

****

Soldiers! Come and take your places under the flags of your leader! He has no existence except in your existence, he has no rights except your rights and those of the people; his interests, his honor, his glory are none other than your interests, your honor, your glory.

****

Victory will march at a quickstep. The eagle and tricolor shall fly from steeple to steeple to

15

the towers of Notre Dame. Then you can show your scars without dishonor, then you can pride yourselves on what you have accomplished: you will be the liberators of the fatherland!

****

In your old age, surrounded and admired by your fellow citizens, who will listen with respect when you tell of your great deeds, you will be able to say with pride, "I, too, was part of that Grand Army which twice entered the walls of Vienna, which cleansed Paris of the pollution that treason and the presence of the enemy had left in it."

****

Russian, Prussian, and German soldiers stay at their posts from a sense of duty; the French soldier, from a sense of honor. The former is almost indifferent to defeat, the latter are humiliated by defeat.

****

Whoever prefers death to ignominy will save his life and live in honor, but he who prefers life will die and cover himself with disgrace.

****

These three things you must always keep in mind: concentration of strength, activity, and a firm resolve to perish gloriously. They are the three principles of the military art which have disposed of luck in my favor in all my operations. Death is nothing, but to live defeated and without glory is to die every day.

BOLDNESS, AUDACITY, AND COURAGE

(According to Napoleon, bold resolutions enable a commander to emerge victorious from an uneven struggle.)

Intelligent and intrepid generals assure the success of actions.

****

When a man has no courage, he necessarily lacks head and is unfit to command either himself or others.

****

At the commencement of a campaign, the question of whether to advance or not requires careful deliberation;

but when you have once undertaken the offensive, it should be maintained to the last extremity.

A retreat, however skillful the maneuvers may be, will always produce an injurious moral effect on the army since by losing the chances of success yourself you throw them into the hands of the enemy.

Besides, retreats cost far more, both in men and material, than the most bloody engagements;

18

with this difference, that in a battle the enemy loses nearly as much as you, while in a retreat the loss is all on your side.

****

A soldier must do his duty without seeking out danger.

****

In giving battle a general should regard it as his first duty to maintain the honor and glory of his arms.
To spare his troops should be but a secondary consideration.
But the same determination and perseverance which promote the former object are the best means of securing the latter.
In a retreat you lose, in addition to the honor of your arms, more men than in two battles.
For this reason, you should never despair while there remain brave men around the colors. This is the conduct which wins and deserves to win, the victory.

****

Turenne is the only general whose boldness increased with age and experience... His last campaigns are superb.

****

A man with neither courage nor bravery is a mere thing.

****

An ordinary general occupying a bad position, if surprised by a superior force, seeks safety in retreat;
but a great captain displays the utmost determination and advances to meet the enemy.
By this movement he disconcerts his adversary;
and if the march of the latter evinces irresolution, an able general, profiting by the moment of indecision, may yet hope for victory or at least employ the day in maneuvering; and at night he can entrench himself or fall back on a better position.
By this fearless conduct, he maintains the honor of his arms, which forms so essential a part of the strength of an army.

****

The first quality of a soldier is constancy in enduring fatigue and hardship. Courage is only the second. Poverty, privation, and want are the school of the good soldier.

****

The effect of discussions, making a show of talent, and calling councils of war will be what the effect of these things has been in every age: they will end in the adoption of the most pusillanimous or (if the expression is preferred) the most prudent measures, which in war are almost uniformly the worst that can be adopted.
True wisdom, so far as a general is concerned, consists in energetic determination.

****

The rabble loves and esteems only those it fears.

****

The human family has two virtues which we cannot value too highly courage in a man, and modesty in a woman.

****

To authorize generals and officers to lay down their arms by virtue of a special capitulation under any other circumstances than when they constitute the garrison of a fortified place, would unquestionably be attended with dangerous consequences.

To open this door to cowards, to men wanting in energy or even to misguided brave men, is to destroy the military spirit of a nation. An extraordinary situation requires extraordinary resolution. The more obstinate the resistance of an armed body, the more chances it will have of being succored or of forcing a passage. How many things apparently impossible have nevertheless been performed by resolute men who had no alternative but death!

****

Hardship, blood, and death create enthusiasts and martyrs and give birth to bold and desperate resolutions.

****

Agreements to surrender made by surrounded bodies, either during a battle or during an active campaign, are contracts with all the advantageous clauses in favor of the individuals who contract them, and all the onerous clauses against the prince and the other soldiers of the army. To avoid peril oneself, while making the position of the rest more dangerous, is an act of cowardice.

****

There is as much true courage in suffering from constancy the despair of the soul, as in standing firm under the fire of a battery

****

Intelligence precedes force. Force itself is nothing without intelligence. In the heroic age the leader was the strongest man; with civilization, he has become the most intelligent of the brave.

****

Alarms dampen spirits and paralyze courage.

****

I value the bravery, fidelity, and loyalty of the Swiss, and this feeling has induced me to decide that all Swiss regiments should consist of Swiss citizens without any mixture of deserters or other foreigners.

****

But these flaws are eclipsed by his great actions, brilliant maneuvers, and bold resolutions that enabled him to emerge victorious from such an uneven struggle.

****

The art of being sometimes audacious and sometimes very prudent is the secret of success. (In 1792) Dumouriez made a very audacious move by positioning himself in the midst of the Prussian army. Even though I am a more audacious warrior than he was, I would not have dared such a maneuver.

****

It is said that I am daring, but Frederick (the Great) was much more so. He was great, especially at the most critical moments. This is the highest praise one could make of his character.

****

Caesar (...) ran great risks in adventures where he demonstrated his boldness. He extracted himself from them through his genius... He was at one and the same time a man of great genius and great audacity.

****

Marshal Ney (...) is a brave man, zealous and all heart. (At Waterloo) he was given the honor of commanding the great attack in the center. It could not have been entrusted to a braver man or one more accustomed to this sort of affair.

****

I loved Murat because of his brilliant bravery, which is why I put up with so much of his foolishness. Like Ney, Murat was incomparable on the field of battle, but he always committed stupid mistakes.

****

For sharp, prolonged attacks that require great boldness, Massena would be more appropriate than Reynier. To protect the kingdom against invasion, Jourdan is preferable to Massena.

****

Henry IV was a good soldier, but in his time war demanded only courage and good sense. It was very different in a war fought with great masses. The bravery that a commander, since his bravery should not resemble that of a grenadier captain.

25

****

The fire of youth, the pride of blood, the death of hope, all produce enthusiasts and martyrs and bring forth courageous and desperate decisions.

****

Glory and the honor of arms is the first duty that a general who delivers battle must consider; the safety and conversation of his men are only secondary. But it is also in his boldness and stubbornness that the safety and conversation of men are found.

****

What is begun in feebleness belongs of right to audacity, which makes it legitimately its own by seizing it.

****

I have very rarely met with that "two o'clock in the morning courage"; in other words, spontaneous courage which is necessary on some unexpected occasion and which permits full freedom of judgment and decision despite the most unforeseen events.

****

With audacity, one can undertake anything, but not do everything.

****

Nor did Frederick violate a second principle no less sacred, that of not abandoning his line of operation. But he changed it, which is considered the most skillful maneuver taught by the art of war. In effect, an army that changes its line of operation from Neumarkt and took that from Upper Silesia. The boldness and the rapidity of execution and the intrepidity of both generals and soldiers were equal to the skill of the maneuver.

****

Fear and uncertainty hasten the fall of empires. They are a thousand times deadlier than the risks and losses of an unsuccessful war.

****

Suicide is the act of a gambler who has lost everything, or of a ruined prodigal. It has always been a maxim with me that a man showed more true courage in supporting the ills of life than by ending it.

****

Citizen Boyer, the surgeon in charge of the wounded at Alexandria, was coward enough to refuse aid to those wounded who had been in contact with patients supposedly struck by contagious diseases. He is unworthy of being a French citizen. He will be dressed up as a woman and led, on a donkey, through the streets of Alexandria, with a sign on his back, reading: Unworthy of being a French citizen: He is afraid of dying.

****

Audacity succeeds as often as it fails; in life, it has an even chance.

****

Caesar had to fight courageous enemies. He took great risks in the adventures into which he was pushed by his boldness; his genius got him out of his difficulties.

****

Caesar (…) was a man whose genius and boldness was equally great.

PLANNING, PREPARATION, AND CALCULATION

(According to Napoleon, the great actions must proceed from a calculation. Also, according to Napoleon, a commander must always be prepared.)

No great actions are the product of chance and luck.

****

A plan of a campaign should anticipate everything which the enemy can do, and contain within itself the means of thwarting him.
Plans of a campaign may be infinitely modified according to the circumstances, the genius of the commander, the quality of the troops and the topography of the theater of war.

****

The great actions must always proceed from calculation and genius.

****

All wars should be systematic, for every war should have an aim and be conducted in conformity with the principles and rules of the art.

War should be undertaken with forces corresponding to the magnitude of the obstacles that are to be anticipated.

****

An army should be every day, every night, and every hour, ready to offer all the resistance of which it is capable.

It is necessary, therefore,

that the soldiers should always have their arms and ammunition at hand;

that the infantry should always have with it its artillery, cavalry, and generals;

that the different divisions of the army should be always in a position to assist, support and protect each other;

that whether encamped, marching or halted, the troops should be always in advantageous positions, possessing the qualities required for every field of battle –

that is to say, the flanks should be well supported and the artillery so placed that it may all be brought into play.

When the army is in a column of march, there must be advanced guards and flank guards to observe the enemy's movements in front, on the right, and on the left;

and at sufficient distances to allow the main body of the arm to deploy and take up its position.

****

One must be slow in deliberation and quick in execution.

****

A general should say to himself many times a day: If the hostile army were to make its appearance in front, on my right, or on my left, what should I do?
And if he is embarrassed, his arrangements are bad; there is something wrong; he must rectify his mistake.

****

In war everything is mental.

****

Among mountains, there are everywhere numerous positions extremely strong by nature, which you should abstain from attacking.

The genius of this kind of war consists in occupying camps either on the flank or the rear of the enemy,

So as to leave him no alternative but to withdraw from his position without fighting, and to move him farther back, or to make him come out and attack you.

In mountain war, the attacking party acts at a disadvantage.

Even in offensive war, the merit lies in having only defensive conflicts and obliging your enemy to become the assailant.

****

Prepare a plan... War consists of unforeseen events.

****

A military maxim, which ought never to be neglected, is to assemble your cantonments at the point which is most remote and best sheltered from the enemy, especially when he makes his appearance unexpectedly.

You will then have time to unite the whole army before he can attack you.

****

In war, it is necessary to have sound and precise ideas. It is with safe and well-conceived plans that we win wars.

****

When you intend to engage in a decisive battle, avail yourself of all the chances of success; more especially if you have to do with a great captain;
for if you are beaten, though you may be in the midst of your magazines and near your fortified posts, woe to the vanquished!

****

With a great general there is never a continuity of great actions which can be attributed to chance and good luck;
they always are the result of calculation and genius.

****

Simply gathering men together does not produce soldiers: drill instruction and skill are what makes real soldiers.

****

No great actions are the product of chance and luck; they must always proceed from calculation and genius. Rarely does one see the great men fail in their most perilous enterprises. Consider Alexander, Caesar, Hannibal, Gustavus Adolphus, and other Great Captains. They always succeeded. It is because there were lucky that they thus became great men? No! But being great men, they knew how master chance. When one desires to study the sources of their success, he is quite astonished to see that they have done everything in obtaining it.

****

Fortune is a woman: if you miss her today, do not expect to find her tomorrow.

****

Alexander, when scarcely more than a small boy and with a mere handful of troops, conquered on a fourth of the globe but was this on his part a simple eruption or an unexpected deluge? No. Everything is profoundly calculated, executed with audacity, and conducted with wisdom.

****

My son should often read and meditate on history; it is the only real philosophy. And he should read and meditate on the campaigns of the Great Captains. This is the only way to learn the art of war.

****

In war, nothing is accomplished except through calculation. Anything that is not profoundly meditated in its details will produce no result.

****

Matters are contemplated over a long period of time and, to attain success, you must devote several months to thinking about what might happen. If I take so many precautions it is because my habit is to leave nothing to chance.

****

A plan of campaign must anticipate everything that the enemy can do and contain within it the means of outmaneuvering him.

****

Plans of a campaign are modified to infinity, according to circumstances, the genius of the commander, the nature of the troops, and the topography.

****

There two kinds of plans for a campaign: good plans and bad plans. Sometimes the good plans fail as a result of accidental circumstances, and occasionally bad ones succeed through some freak of fortune.

****

I am in the habit of thinking three or four months in advance about what I must do, and to master the secrets of the art of war.

****

Intelligent and intrepid generals assure the success of actions. One must be slow in deliberation and quick in execution. To win is not enough: it is necessary to profit from success. In the profession of war, like that of letters, each has his style.

****

In a war of this nature, we must be composed, patient, and calculating. We must not exhaust the troops in needless marches and countermarches. We must not assume that when we have made one false march of three or four days that we could make up for it by countermarch this is usually committing two mistakes instead of one.

****

At the moment war is declared there is so much to do that it is wise to begin preparation several years in advance.

****

I calculate on the basis of the worst possible case. If I take so many precautions it is because my custom is to leave nothing to chance.

****

There is no man more pusillanimous than I when it comes to planning a campaign. I purposely exaggerate all the dangers and all the calamities that the circumstances make possible. I am in a thoroughly painful state of agitation. This does not keep me from looking quite serene in front of my entourage; I am like an unmarried girl laboring with a child. Once I have made up my mind, everything is forgotten except what leads to success.

****

The ideal army would be the one in which every officer would know what he ought to do in every contingency; the best possible army is the one that comes closest to this.

****

In war, nothing can be gained except by calculation. Whatever has not been profoundly meditated in all its details is totally ineffectual.

****

Military science consists in first calculating all the possibilities accurately and then in making an almost mathematically exact allowance for an accident. It is on this point that one must make no mistake; a decimal more or less may alter everything.

****

Being great men, they knew how to master chance.

****

Now, this apportioning of knowledge and accident can take place only in the head of a genius, for without it there can be no creation – and surely the greatest improvisation of the human mind is that which gives existence to the nonexistent. Accident thus always remains a mystery to mediocre and becomes reality for superior men.

****

The ignorant suspect no difficulties. They want to solve a problem of transcendental mathematics by means of a second-degree formula.

****

All questions of grand tactics are indeterminate physicomathematical equations that are incapable of solution by formulas of elementary mathematics.

CIRCUMSTANCES AND FLEXIBILITY

(According to Napoleon, the plan must be modified according to the circumstances and therefore, a commander must be flexible! Also, according to Napoleon, a commander must profit by circumstances.)

Since the war depends absolutely on the season, each month requires a different plan of campaign.

****

A plan of a campaign should anticipate everything which the enemy can do, and contain within itself the means of thwarting him.
Plans of a campaign may be infinitely modified according to the circumstances, the genius of the commander, the quality of the troops and the topography of the theater of war.

****

Conquerors should know the genius and the language of every religion. They ought to be Moslems in Egypt and Catholics in France, to the extent, at least, of giving sympathetic protection.

41

****

Fortune is a woman: if you miss her today, do not expect to find her tomorrow.

****

Conditions of the ground should not alone decide the organization for combat,
which should be determined from a consideration of all circumstances.

****

The geographical conditions of a country, life in plains or mountains, education or discipline, have more influence than climate on the character of the troops.

****

In politics nothing is immutable. Events carry within them an invincible power. The unwise destroy themselves in resistance. The skillful accept events, take strong hold of them and direct them.

****

Those who cannot profit by circumstances are ninnies.

****

All great captains have done great things only by conforming to the rules and natural principles of the art;
that is to say, by the wisdom of their combinations, the reasoned balance of means with consequences, and efforts with obstacles.
They have succeeded only by thus conforming, whatever may have been the audacity of their enterprises and the extent of their success.
They have never ceased to make war a veritable science.

****

It is only under this title that they are our great models, and it is only in imitating them that one can hope to approach them.

****

-In the art of war - there are no precise or fixed rules. Everything depends upon the character that nature has bestowed upon the general, on his qualities and faults, on the character of troops, on the range of arms, on the season, and on a thousand circumstances that are never the same.

Another translation:
There are no precise, determinate rules: everything depends on the character that nature has bestowed on the general, on his qualities and defects, on the nature of the troops, on the range of the weapons, on the season of the year, and on a thousand circumstances which are never twice the same.

****

It is known that I did not insist on bending circumstances to my ideas, but that, as a general rule, I let myself influenced by them.

****

Man achieves in life only by commanding the capabilities nature has given him, or by creating them within himself by education and by knowing how to profit by the difficulties encountered.

****

But who can, in advance, respond to fortuitous circumstances or unexpected events? How many times, therefore, have I been forced to completely change (my plan). Also, I have acted from general principles far more than from resolved plans.

****

Lead the ideas of your time and they will accompany and support you; fall behind them and they drag you along with them; oppose them and they will overwhelm you.

****

My greatest deeds have been attributed to luck, and people will not fail to charge my reverses to my shortcomings,
but if I were to write about my campaigns people would indeed be astonished to see that in both instances my judgment and abilities were always exercised only in conformity with principles.

****

Events all hang by a hair. The clever man profits by everything, neglecting nothing that may give him an advantage. The less clever, by slighting some seeming trifle, loses all.

****

All these Great Captains of Antiquity (...) and those who, much later, have deservedly marched in their footsteps, have performed great deeds only by conforming to the rules and the natural principles of the art of war – in other words, by the precision of the combinations and the intelligent relationship between ends and means, and of efforts with obstacles.

****

I waged the campaign without consulting anyone. I could not have done it well had I been forced to reconcile my point of view with that of another.

****

Plans of a campaign are modified to infinity, according to circumstances, the genius of the commander, the nature of the troops, and the topography.

****

War is composed of nothing but accidents, and, although holding to general principles, a general should never lose sight of everything to enable him to profit from these accidents; that is the mark of genius.

In war there is but one favorable moment; the great art is to seize it.

****

Your Majesty's family ties with Russia signify nothing. The intentions of Emperor Alexander's court mean just as little. Among great nations, facts alone speak; the trend of public opinion determines the events... If the emperor wants war, the trend of public opinion agrees with his intentions; if he does not want war and does not promptly halt that impetus, he will be dragged into it against his will next year. This war will come despite me, despite him, despite the interests of France and of Russia. I have seen this happen so often that my experience of the past reveals these future events to me... Your Majesty could not possibly suppose that I want war. Why should I?

****

The war consists of nothing but accidents and that a commander, though he must always adjust himself to general principles, should never overlook anything that might enable him to exploit these accidents. The vulgar would call this luck, but in fact, it is the characteristic of genius.

****

Sometimes a single battle decides everything, and sometimes, too, the slightest circumstance decides the issue of a battle.

****

In revolutions, there are only two sorts of men, those who cause them and those who profit by them.

****

In order to weigh the merits of generals, the quality of their troops and of those of the enemy must be taken into consideration.

CONCENTRATION AND CENTER OF GRAVITY

(According to Napoleon, a commander must concentrate his forces on a single point.)

It is the same with strategy as with the siege of a fortress: concentrate your fire against a single point, and once the wall is breached all of the rest becomes worthless and the fortress is captured. It is Germany that must be crushed; once this is accomplished Spain and Italy will fall by themselves. Therefore it is essential not to scatter our attacks but to concentrate them.

****

The art consists, with an inferior army, of always having more forces than your enemy at the point where you attack, or at the point which is attacked; but this art cannot be learned either from books or from practice. It is a feeling of command which properly constitutes the genius for war.

****

It may be laid down as a principle that in invading a country with two or three armies,

each of which has its own distinct line of operations extending towards a fixed point at which all are to unite, the union of the different corps should never be ordered to take place in the vicinity of the enemy,
as by concentrating his forces he may not only prevent their junction but also defeat them one by one.

****

It is a violation of correct principles to cause corps to act separately, without communication with each other, in the face of a concentrated army with easy communications.

****

Gustavus Adolphus, Turenne, and Frederic, as also Alexander, Hannibal, and Caesar have all acted on the same principles.
To keep your forces united,
to be vulnerable at no point,
to bear down with rapidity upon important points –
these are the principles which ensure victory.

****

When you are driven from your first position, the rallying point of your columns should be so far in the rear that the enemy cannot get there before them.

It would be the greatest of disasters to have your columns attacked one by one before their reunion.

****

When you have it in contemplation to give battle, it is a general rule to collect all your strength and to leave none unemployed.

One battalion sometimes decides the issue of the day.

****

Nothing is more important in war than unity in command.

When, therefore, you are carrying on hostilities against a single power only, you should have but one army acting on one line and led by one commander.

****

Your great task is to keep all your forces together and to reach Naples as quickly as possible with your entire command... Never hold a council of war, but listen to the views of each in private... Prince Eugene, who commands in the Kingdom of Italy, will hold a reserve ready to meet any unexpected event.

****

I repeat: do not divide your forces. Let your entire army pass the Apennines and your three corps march against Naples, positioned in such a way that they can be united on the same battlefield in a single day.

****

In a battle like in a siege, skill consists in converging a mass of fire on a single point:
Once the combat is opened, the commander who is adroit will suddenly and unexpectedly open fire with a surprising mass of artillery on one of these points, and is sure to seize it.

****

A general who retains fresh troops for the day after a battle is almost always beaten.
He should, if helpful, throw in his last man, because on the day after a complete success there are no more obstacles in front of him;
prestige alone will ensure new triumphs to the conqueror.
An army composed of men in different nations will not hesitate to commit foolish mistakes...

The military art would be to expect these mistakes and to benefit from them.

****

When you occupy a position which the enemy threatens to surround, you should collect your forces quickly and menace him with an offensive movement.

By this maneuver, you prevent him from detaching a part of his troops and annoying your flanks, in case you should deem a retreat indispensable.

****

Greeks in the service of Alexander the Great felt no passion for his cause. The Swiss in the service of France, Spain, and of some Italian princes had no passion for their cause. Frederick the Great's troops, composed in large measure of foreigners, had no passion for his cause.

****

Unity of command is of the first necessity in war. You must keep the army united, concentrate as many of your troops as possible on the battlefield, and take advantage of every opportunity, for fortune is a woman: if you miss her today, do not expect to find her tomorrow.

****

If you weaken your means by dividing your forces, or break the unity of military thought in Italy... you will have lost the most favorable occasion for imposing laws on Italy.

****

You will employ all the demonstrations and appearances of movement that you judge convenient to deceive the enemy about the real strategical objective and persuade him that he will first be attacked by you. Therefore exaggerate your forces and announce immense and near reinforcements approaching from the interior.

Finally, you will mislead the enemy, insofar as it is possible, about the true points of attack, which are the Saint-Gotthard and the Simplon.

****

In the Moravian campaign (1806) I understood that the Russians, having no general of the first rank, would believe that the French army would retreat upon Vienna. They had to make it a high priority to intercept this road, when in fact the retreat of the army throughout the Moravian campaign had never been intended to be toward Vienna. This single circumstance distorted all of the enemy's calculations and inevitably contributed to those movements that led to his defeat.

****

The issue of a battle is the result of a single thought.

****

The art of war consists, with a numerically inferior army, in always having larger forces than the enemy at the point which is to be attacked or defended.

****

My great and most distinctive talent is to see everything in a clear light; even my eloquence is of the kind which sees the core of each question from all its facets at once – like the perpendicular, which is shorter than the diagonal.

COORDINATION AND COMMUNICATION

(According to Napoleon, a commander must not allow corps to act separately, without communication with each other. Also, according to Napoleon, the coordination comes from communication.)

It may be laid down as a principle that in invading a country with two or three armies, each of which has its own distinct line of operations extending towards a fixed point at which all are to unite, the union of the different corps should never be ordered to take place in the vicinity of the enemy,
as by concentrating his forces he may not only prevent their junction but also defeat them one by one.

****

An army should be every day, every night, and every hour, ready to offer all the resistance of which it is capable.
It is necessary, therefore,
that the soldiers should always have their arms and ammunition at hand;
that the infantry should always have with it its artillery, cavalry, and generals;

that the different divisions of the army should be always in a position to assist, support and protect each other;

that whether encamped, marching or halted, the troops should be always in advantageous positions, possessing the qualities required for every field of battle –

that is to say, the flanks should be well supported and the artillery so placed that it may all be brought into play.

When the army is in a column of march, there must be advanced guards and flank guards to observe the enemy's movements in front, on the right, and on the left;

and at sufficient distances to allow the main body of the arm to deploy and take up its position.

****

It is a violation of correct principles to cause corps to act separately, without communication with each other, in the face of a concentrated army with easy communications.

****

The camps of the same army should be always so placed as to be able to sustain each other.

****

Infantry, cavalry, and artillery cannot dispense with each other.
They ought to be quartered in such a manner as always to be able to support each other in case of surprise.

****

The first law of naval tactics should be that as soon as the admiral has given the signal that he is going to attack, each captain should make the necessary movements to attack an enemy ship, take part in the combat and support his neighbors.

****

The success of an army and its well-being depend essentially upon order and discipline, which will make us loved by the people who come to greet us and with whom we share enemies. Pillaging destroys everything, even the army that practices it.

****

However, the real army was formed en route. The divisions were organized at different points of rendezvous. These places were isolated and had no connection to each other...

The most difficult thing to conceal was the movement of needed provisions through arid mountains where nothing could be found.

****

The best generals will be those who move up from the field artillery. It is the duty of an artillery general to understand all of the operations of the army, insofar as he is forced to provide the different divisions with arms and ammunition. His contacts with the individual battery commander in each division enable him to know everything that is going on.

VELOCITY AND NOT LOSING TIME

(According to Napoleon, the rapidity increases the means of the victory. Also, according to Napoleon, in war every delay is fatal.)

The strength of an army, like the momentum in mechanics, is estimated by the weight multiplied by the velocity.
A rapid march exerts a beneficial moral influence on the army and increases its means of victory.

****

Great operations (...) require speed in movements and as much quickness in conception as in execution... We require therefore unity of thought – military, diplomatic, and financial.

****

When your army is inferior in numbers, inferior in cavalry and in artillery, a pitched battle should be avoided.
The want of numbers must be supplied by rapidity in marching;
the want of artillery by the character of the maneuvers;

the inferiority in cavalry by the choice of positions.

In such a situation, it is of great importance that confidence should prevail among the soldiers.

****

Commanders-in-chief are to be guided by their own experience or genius.

Tactics, evolutions and the science of the engineer and the artillery officer may be learned from treatises,

but generalship is acquired only by experience and the study of the campaigns of all great captains.

Gustavus Adolphus, Turenne, and Frederic, as also Alexander, Hannibal, and Caesar have all acted on the same principles.

To keep your forces united,

to be vulnerable at no point,

to bear down with rapidity upon important points –

these are the principles which ensure victory.

****

Wartime is not the same as peacetime. In war every delay is fatal. Manifestly you need order, but this order must be of a different kind in times of peace.

****

In his Civil War campaigns, Caesar triumphed by following the same methods and principles, but he ran far greater risks. He crossed the Rubicon with only a single legion, seized thirty cohorts at Corfinium, and drove Pompey from Italy in three months. What swiftness! What suddenness! What audacity!

****

The loss of time is irreparable in war. The reasons that one gives are always poor because operations misfire only through delays. The art consists simply of gaining time when one has inferior forces.

****

I notice with pain that you do not march with suitable energy. You are the commander in chief; you must remove all difficulties... Everything you do will be well done provided you are soon victorious. March rapidly and vigorously without any but, if, or because. The special affection that I have for you has caused me to decide to let you acquire this glory. Be of firm character and will...

****

Nor did Frederick violate a second principle no less sacred, that of not abandoning his line of operation. But he changed it, which is considered the most skillful maneuver taught by the art of war. In effect, an army that changes its line of operation from Neumarkt and took that from Upper Silesia. The boldness and the rapidity of execution and the intrepidness of both generals and soldiers were equal to the skill of the maneuver.

DECEPTION, SURPRISE AND EXAGGERATING YOUR FORCES

(According to Napoleon, in war, in order to surprise an enemy, deception is a must! Also, according to Napoleon, a commander must always exaggerate the numbers of his forces.)

A well-established maxim of war is not to do anything which your enemy wishes and for the single reason that he does so wish.

You should, therefore, avoid a field of battle which he has reconnoitered and studied.

You should be still more careful to avoid one which he has fortified and where he has entrenched himself.

A corollary of this principle is, never to attack in front a position which admits of being turned.

****

When you occupy a position which the enemy threatens to surround, you should collect your forces quickly and menace him with an offensive movement.

By this maneuver, you prevent him from detaching a part of his troops and annoying your flanks, in case you should deem a retreat indispensable.

****

Tell him that when he is induced to reveal the strength of his forces he should exaggerate and present them as formidable by doubling or trebling the number and that when he mentions the enemy he should diminish his force by half or one third.

****

In war everything is mental, and the King strayed from this principle when he stated that he had only 40,000 men and proclaimed that the insurgents have 120,000. This discourages the French troops by representing enemy numbers as immense and gives the enemy a poor opinion of the French by proclaiming his weakness throughout Spain.

****

In brief, it gives moral strength to his enemies and takes it away from himself. Man is naturally inclined to believe that in the long run numbers must be defeated by greater numbers.

****

On the day of battle the best-trained soldiers have difficulty in evaluating the number of men in the enemy army, and in general, it is a natural instinct to be inclined to see the enemy as being larger in numbers than he actually is.

****

But when one has the imprudence to allow... exaggerated estimates of enemy strength... every cavalry colonel on reconnaissance sees an army, and each light infantry captain sees whole battalions...

****

In war, intellect and judgment are the better part of reality. The art of the Great Captains has always been to (...) make their own forces appear to be very large to the enemy and to make the enemy view themselves as being very inferior...

****

When I defeated the Austrian army at Eckmuhl, I was outnumbered five to one, and yet my soldiers believed that they were at least equal in strength to the enemy. Even today, despite the long time that has elapsed since we were in Germany, the enemy does not know our real strength. We make a point of making our numbers appear larger every day. Far from admitting that I had only 100,000 at Wagram, I continue to pretend that I had 220,000 men.

****

And constantly in my Italian campaigns, where I had a handful of everything, I exaggerated my strength. That served my plans and did not diminish my glory.

****

My generals and the trained soldiers know well – after the event – how to recognize all of the capacity of operations, even that of having exaggerated the numbers of my troops.

****

In Egypt, I had agreed with all of the colonels that, in the Orders of the Day, we would inflate by one third the real quantity of the total distribution of provisions, arms, and clothing. Thus the author of the Military Precis of the Campaign of 1789 was astonished to learn that the Orders of the Day for this army had shown its strength to be 40,000 when other authentic information that he had received gave its effective strength as far less. In the reports of the Italian campaigns of 1796 and 1797, and since, the same means have been used to give exaggerated ideas of French strengths.

****

The most suitable way (...) was to reveal it myself by making such a demonstration that it would become an object of ridicule to the enemy, and to act in such a way that the enemy considered all of these declarations as a way to create a diversion to the operations of the Austrian army, which blocked Genoa. It was necessary to give a specific objective to the observers and spies.

****

The combination of all of these means of putting the spies on the wrong scent was crowded with the most fortunate success.

****

The French count too much on our naivete; they would have us read like the fabled dow who leaves his prey for a mere shadow.

****

You know very well (...) the importance of the most profound secrecy in such circumstances... You will employ all the demonstrations and appearances of movement that you judge convenient to deceive the enemy about the real strategical objective and persuade him that he will first be attacked by you. Therefore exaggerate your forces and announce immense and near reinforcements approaching from the interior.

Finally, you will mislead the enemy, insofar as it is possible, about the true points of attack, which are the Saint-Gotthard and the Simplon.

DISCIPLINE

(According to Napoleon, without discipline there is no victory.)

Without discipline, there is no victory.

****

A good general, a good officer, commissioned and non-commissioned, good organization, good instruction and strict discipline make good troops independently of the cause for which they are fighting.
But enthusiasm, love of country and the desire of contributing to the national glory may also animate young troops with advantage.

****

Military discipline admits of no modification.

****

The success of an army and its well-being depend essentially upon order and discipline.

****

It is urgent that we get rid of all soldiers unfit for service and who must be fed and supplied without being useful.

****

Military discipline admits of no modification. The army must understand that discipline, wisdom, and the respect for property support its victories, that pillage and theft belong only to the cowardly, who are unworthy of remaining in the ranks (...) that they plot the loss of their honor and that they have no goal other than to stain the laurels acquired by so much bravery and perseverance. Without discipline, there is no victory.

****

Russian troops are brave, but far less so than the French: the experience of their generals and the ignorance and sluggishness of their soldiers make their armies actually less formidable.

****

The success of an army and its well-being depend essentially upon order and discipline, which will make us loved by the people who come to greet us and with whom we share enemies. Pillaging destroys everything, even the army that practices it.

****

When I arrived (in Italy in 1796) the army was injured by the bad influence of the troublemakers: it lacked bread, discipline, and subordination. I made some examples, devoted all of our means to reviving the administrative services of the army, and victory did the rest... Without bread, the soldier tends to an excess of violence that makes one blush for being a man.

****

We will never forget to make a disciplinary example of these soldiers who deviate from the rule of severe discipline.

****

When you issue orders, take measures to assure that they are executed and punish those who commit such a serious fault.

****

Why repeat an order? An order must always be carried out; when it is not, it is a crime and the guilty man must be punished.

****

The conduct of generals is more delicate after battles than before because then, having been able to pursue only one course, they find themselves criticized by everybody who favored other alternatives.

****

I would certainly desire that the canaille (...) revolt. As long as you have not made an example of anyone you will never be master.

****

All persons who have committed excesses, and stirred up rebellion, either by setting up any rallying signal for the crowd, or by exciting it against the French, or the government, must be brought before a military tribunal and instantly shot. Two or three examples are indispensable and must be made. Every spy... (and) every leader of a riot must be shot.

****

As a general rule, it is a political principle to create a good impression of your benevolence after having demonstrated that you can be severe with troublemakers. Get rid of the prominent men; punish the smallest fault with severity.

****

All foreign people, but especially the Italians, need severe repression from time to time. There is no doubt that you have nothing to fear from the moneyed classes, but... the ignorance of the mountain people is such that they interpret the absence of punishment as weakness and (...) the consequences of this are always very dangerous.

****

Make the grandees and other influential people of the country understand thoroughly that the fate of (...) the country (...) depends on their behavior. Hostages are one of the most effective ways to (...) keep conquered provinces under control (...) when the people are persuaded that the death of these hostages would be the immediate result of a breach of their loyalty.

****

The chief virtues of a soldier are constancy and discipline. Valor comes only in second place.

****

The Emperor asserted that the only way of keeping soldiers to their duty was to drive them with blows. I cited the example of the Germans, who are led in that manner and whom our soldiers have always defeated. His Majesty wants order and discipline everywhere. "Look at the English! And sure enough, they have defeated us although they are undoubtedly inferior to our soldiers!"

****

All goes well. There is less looting... The wretches (the looters) are excusable: after languishing for three years on the crest of the Alps, they came into the promised land and wanted to taste of its fruits. I had three of them shot and sent six more back to break stones beyond the Var.

DETERMINATION, CONSTANCY, AND RESOLUTION

(According to Napoleon, how many things apparently impossible have nevertheless been performed by resolute men who had no alternative but death! Also, according to Napoleon, The first quality of a soldier is constancy in enduring fatigue and hardship.)

The first quality of a soldier is constancy in enduring fatigue and hardship. Courage is only the second.

Poverty, privation, and want are the schools of the good soldier.

****

The effect of discussions, making a show of talent, and calling councils of war will be what the effect of these things has been in every age: they will end in the adoption of the most pusillanimous or (if the expression is preferred) the most prudent measures, which in war are almost uniformly the worst that can be adopted.

True wisdom, so far as a general is concerned, consists in energetic determination.

****

The essential quality of a general is firmness.

****

There are certain things in a war of which the commander alone comprehends the importance.
Nothing but his superior firmness and ability can subdue and surmount all difficulties.

****

Nothing is so rare as steadfast devotion.

****

There is as much true courage in suffering from constancy the despair of the soul, as in standing firm under the fire of a battery.

****

To authorize generals and officers to lay down their arms by virtue of a special capitulation under any other circumstances than when they constitute the garrison of a fortified place, would unquestionably be attended with dangerous consequences.

To open this door to cowards, to men wanting in energy or even to misguided brave men, is to destroy the military spirit of a nation.

****

An extraordinary situation requires extraordinary resolution.

****

The more obstinate the resistance of an armed body, the more chances it will have of being succored or of forcing a passage.

****

How many things apparently impossible have nevertheless been performed by resolute men who had no alternative but death!

****

The first principle of a general-in-chief is to calculate what he must do,
to see if he has all the means to surmount the obstacles with which the enemy can oppose him and,
when he has made his decision, to do everything to overcome them.

****

A general-in-chief should never allow any rest either to the conquerors or to the conquered.

****

An irresolute general who acts without principles and without a plan,
even though he leads an army numerically superior to that of the enemy,
almost always finds himself inferior to the latter on the field of battle.
Fumblings, the mezzo termine (the middle course) lose all in war.

****

In war the commander of a fortress is not a judge of events; he should defend the fortress to the last;
he deserves death if he surrenders it a moment before he is forced to.

****

We need men and not boys. No one is braver than our young people, but lacking fortitude they fill the hospitals and even at the slightest uncertainty they show the character of their age.

****

In war, only the commander understands the importance of certain things, and he alone, through his will and superior insight, conquers and surmounts all difficulties.

****

The essential quality of a general is firmness... which is a gift from heaven. (In the campaign of 1800 in Germany) Moreau, three times in forty days, repeated the same demonstrations, but every time without giving them the appearance of reality. He succeeded only in emboldening his enemy and he offered him occasions to strike the isolated divisions... During this campaign, the French army, which was the more numerous, was nearly always inferior in numbers on the battlefield. That is what happens to generals who are irresolute and act without principles and plans.

****

In war tentative measures (...) lose everything. Military genius is a gift from heaven (...) but the most essential quality for a general is firmness of character and the resolution to conquer at any price.

****

A division commander in the Army of Italy, Massena... had a strong constitution and was tireless, on his horse night and day among the boulders and in the mountains. This was the kind of war that he understood particularly well.

****

Massena was determined, brave, bold, full of ambition and vanity. His distinctive characteristic was stubbornness, and he never got discouraged.

****

Berthier was very active and followed his general on all reconnaissances without neglecting any of his work at the bureau. He possessed an indecisive character and was little fit for command, but he had all the qualities of a good chief of staff.

****

Glory and the honor of arms is the first duty that a general who delivers battle must consider; the safety and conversation of his men are only secondary. But it is also in his boldness and stubbornness that the safety and conversation of men are found.

****

In war good health is indispensable. For it is at night when the commander must do his work. If he tires himself unduly during the day fatigue will overcome him at night.

****

At Vitoria, we were defeated because Joseph (Bonaparte) slept too much. Had I slept the night before Eckmuhl I would never have carried out this superb maneuver, which is the most beautiful that I have ever made... My activity enabled me to be everywhere... A commander should not sleep.

****

War is waged only with vigor, decision, and unshaken will. One must neither grope nor hesitate.

****

I notice with pain that you do not march with suitable energy. You are the commander in chief; you must remove all difficulties... Everything you do will be well done provided you are soon victorious. March rapidly and vigorously without any but, if, or because. The special affection that I have for you has caused me to decide to let you acquire this glory. Be of firm character and will...

****

Overcome all obstacles. I will disapprove your actions only if they are fainthearted and irresolute. Everything that is vigorous, firm, and discreet will meet with my approval.

****

The chief virtues of a soldier are constancy and discipline. Valor comes only in second place.

****

If valor is the soldier's first virtue, constancy is the second.

PAYING ATTENTION TO DETAIL

(According to Napoleon, the slightest circumstance decides the issue of a battle. Therefore, a commander must pay attention to details.)

Do not be surprised at the attention that I devote to details: I must pay attention to everything so as never to leave myself unprovided.

****

I must have precise information to adjust my movement and formulate my plan. I need to have very detailed information, to know the width and length of islands, the elevations of mountains, the width of canals... the nature of fortified cities, fortress by fortress, (and) the condition of roads... All of this interests me in the highest degree.

****

I recommend that you take pleasure in reading your muster rolls.

****

The good condition of my armies stems from the fact that I devote an hour or two each day, and when the muster rolls of my troops and my fleets, comprising twenty large volumes, are sent to me each month,

****

I set aside every other task to read the muster rolls in detail and to note any changes in them from one month to the next.

****

I get more pleasure from this kind of reading (reading the muster rolls) than a young girl gets from reading a novel.

****

I advise you to devote one hour every morning to reading your muster rolls in order to know the position of all the units in your army.

****

-Instead of having men beaten who are suspected of having important secrets - study the country: local knowledge is a precious knowledge that sooner or later you will encounter again.

****

There are five things which a soldier ought never to be without his musket, his cartridge-box, his knapsack, his provisions for at least four days and his pioneer hatchet.
Reduce his knapsack, if you deem it necessary to do so, to the smallest size, but let the soldier always have it with him.

****

To be familiar with the geography and topography of the country;
to be skillful in making a reconnaissance;
to be attentive to the despatch of orders;
to be capable of exhibiting with simplicity the most complicated movements of an army –
these are the qualifications that should distinguish the officer called to the station of the chief of the staff.

****

Your letter tells me nothing. You will however have to be able to interrogate in order to know the names of the regiments and the commanding general and a hundred things, all very important – the morale of the troops, the way in which they are fed, the strength of the different units, and what is known from conversations with the colonels and officers of the corps. I expected several pages and I get only two lines. Redeem all that by writing to me in great detail.

****

Military science consists in first calculating all the possibilities accurately and then in making an almost mathematically exact allowance for an accident. It is on this point that one must make no mistake; a decimal more or less may alter everything.

****

Sometimes a single battle decides everything, and sometimes, too, the slightest circumstance decides the issue of a battle.

COOL HEAD, SOUND REASONING, AND SOUND JUDGMENT

(According to Napoleon, the foremost quality of a commander is to keep a cool head, to receive accurate impressions of what is happening. Also, according to Napoleon, a commander must never fret or be amazed or intoxicated by good news or bad.)

The first qualification of a general-in-chief is to possess a cool head so that things may appear to him in their true proportions and as they really are.

He should not suffer himself to be unduly affected by the good or bad news.

The impressions which are made upon his mind successively or simultaneously in the course of a day should be so classified in his memory that each shall occupy its proper place;

for sound reasoning and judgment result from first examining each of these varied impressions by itself, and then comparing them all with one another.

****

There are some men who, from their physical and moral constitution, deck everything in the colors of imagination.

****

With whatever knowledge, talents, courage or other good qualities these may be endowed, nature has not fitted them for the command of armies and the direction of the great operations of war.

****

The soldier cannot judge, but the intelligent officer, whose judgment is fairly and who has knowledge of affairs, pays little attention to the Orders of the Day and to proclamations and knows how to evaluate events...

****

My generals and the trained soldiers know well – after the event – how to recognize all of the capacity of operations, even that of having exaggerated the numbers of my troops.

****

Without this establishment (...) it would be a long time before soldiers possessed the means of learning how to benefit from mistakes that have caused reverses or to appreciate the dispositions that could have prevented them.

****

The successive or simultaneous sensations that the commander's mind receives during the course of a day are classified and occupy only as much attention as they deserve, for common sense and good judgment are products of a comparison of several sensations considered.

****

There are men who, because of their physical and moral makeup, distort a picture of everything. No matter how much knowledge, intellect, courage, and other good qualities they might have, nature has not called upon them to command armies or to direct the great operations of war.

****

As for bedding down with a woman... my woman could have died in Munich or Strasburg and it would not have upset my projects or views by a quarter of an hour.

****

Massena's conversation was not very interesting, but at the first cannon shot, in the midst of bullets and dangers, his thought would acquire strength and clarity. If defeated he would start again as if he had been the victor.

****

Lannes was wise, prudent and bold. In the presence of the enemy, he possessed imperturbable sangfroid. He had little education but real natural ability.

****

On the battlefield, Lannes was superior to all of the French generals when it came to maneuvering 15,000 men. He was still young and he would have continued to improve; perhaps he would have been clever even at Grand Tactics.

****

Give your orders in such a way that they cannot be disobeyed. Carefully explain (...) that they are not susceptible of any but, if, or because; and that twenty-four hours after the orders are received these regiments must be on the move.

****

In a war of this nature, we must be composed, patient, and calculating. We must not exhaust the troops in needless marches and countermarches. We must not assume that when we have made one false march of three or four days that we could make up for it by countermarch this is usually committing two mistakes instead of one.

****

The foremost quality of a general in chief is to keep a cool head, receiving accurate impressions from objects, and never yielding to overexcitement or being dazzled or intoxicated by the good or bad news.

Another translation:
The foremost quality of a commander is to keep a cool head, to receive accurate impressions of what is happening, and never fret or be amazed or intoxicated by good news or bad.

****

SIMPLICITY

(According to Napoleon, the art of war is like everything that is beautiful and simple. The simplest moves are the best. Also, according to Napoleon, his great and most distinctive talent is to see the core of each problem from all its facets.)

To be familiar with the geography and topography of the country;
to be skillful in making a reconnaissance;
to be attentive to the despatch of orders;
to be capable of exhibiting with simplicity the most complicated movements of an army –
these are the qualifications that should distinguish the officer called to the station of the chief of the staff.

****

When the army marches, the geographical engineers, who will have reconnoitered the country, will always be at headquarters in memoranda should always be written in the simplest style and be purely descriptive. They should never stray from their objective by introducing extraneous ideas. An accurate method is the only one that pleases the Emperor.

****

Success in war depends upon the prudence, good conduct, and experience of the general. You do not require spirit in war, but exactitude, character, and simplicity.

****

Berthier knew topography well, understood reconnaissance detachments, attended personally to the expedition of orders, and was accustomed to briefing the most complicated movements of an army with simplicity.

****

The art of war is like everything that is beautiful and simple. The simplest moves are the best. If Macdonald (one of Napoleon's generals), instead of doing whatever he did, had asked a peasant for the way to Genoa, the peasant would have answered, "Through Bobbio" – and that would have been a superb move.

****

My great and most distinctive talent is to see everything in a clear light; even my eloquence is of the kind which sees the core of each question from all its facets at once – like the perpendicular, which is shorter than the diagonal.

INTELLIGENCE AND GETTING PRECISE INFORMATION

(According to Napoleon, in order to get detailed information, a commander must study the problem from every angle. Intelligence is crucial.)

I must have precise information to adjust my movement and formulate my plan. I need to have very detailed information, to know the width and length of islands, the elevations of mountains, the width of canals... the nature of fortified cities, fortress by fortress, (and) the condition of roads... All of this interests me in the highest degree.

****

I recommend that you take pleasure in reading your muster rolls.

****

The good condition of my armies stems from the fact that I devote an hour or two each day, and when the muster rolls of my troops and my fleets, comprising twenty large volumes, are sent to me each month,

****

I set aside every other task to read the muster rolls in detail and to note any changes in them from one month to the next.

****

I get more pleasure from this kind of reading than a young girl gets from reading a novel.

****

I advise you to devote one hour every morning to reading your muster rolls in order to know the position of all the units in your army.

****

To reconnoiter rapidly defiles and fords;
to obtain guides that can be relied upon;
to interrogate the clergyman and the postmaster;
to establish speedily an understanding with the inhabitants;
to send out spies;
to seize the letters in the mails,
to translate and make an abstract of their contents;
in short, to answer all the inquiries of the general-in-chief on his arrival with the whole army - such are the duties which come within

the sphere of a good general of an advanced post.

****

-When pillaging, - The inhabitants leave, which has the dual drawback of turning them into irreconcilable enemies who take revenge upon the isolated soldier, and of swelling the enemy ranks in proportion to the damage that we do. This deprives us of all intelligence, so necessary for waging war, and of every means of subsistence. Peasants, who come to peddle provisions are put off by the troops who stop them, pillage their wares, and beat them?

****

The barbarous custom of having men beaten who are suspected of having important secrets to reveal must be abolished. It has always been recognized that this way of interrogating men, by putting them to torture, produces nothing worthwhile. The poor wretches say anything that comes into their mind and what they think the interrogator wishes to know.

****

-Instead of having men beaten who are suspected of having important secrets - study the country: local knowledge is a precious knowledge that sooner or later you will encounter again.

****

In war, spies and inquires count for nothing: that would be to risk the lives of men on very poor estimates that cannot be trusted.

****

Your letter tells me nothing. You will however have to be able to interrogate in order to know the names of the regiments and the commanding general and a hundred things, all very important – the morale of the troops, the way in which they are fed, the strength of the different units, and what is known from conversations with the colonels and officers of the corps. I expected several pages and I get only two lines. Redeem all that by writing to me in great detail.

****

It is always asserted that we do not have intelligence, as if this situation were extraordinary in an army and it was a routine matter to find spies. In Spain, like everywhere else, we must send detachments sometimes to seize either the cure, or the acolyte, occasionally the head of a convent or the postmaster, and especially to confiscate all letters and sometimes even to seize the mail carrier.

****

Place them under arrest until they talk, by having them interrogated twice a day. Hold them as hostages and charge them with giving information to the enemy. When you know how to take forceful and energetic measures, you will get information. You must intercept all the mail...

****

When I ask for a reconnaissance I do not want someone to give me a plan of campaign. The word enemy must not be used by the engineer! He must reconnoiter the roads, their condition, the slopes, the heights, the gorges, and the obstacles, and verify if the vehicles could cross there, and completely forgo any plans of a campaign...

****

Two or three engineers will be assigned to each of these reconnaissances: they will study the country thoroughly. Two or three engineers will be charged with each of these reconnaissances.

****

I have devoted enough interest to geography to know that there is not a single man to be found in Paris who is perfectly informed of the discoveries that occur each year and the changes that happen incessantly.

****

Do not be surprised at the attention that I devote to details: I must pay attention to everything so as never to leave myself unprovided.

****

The foremost quality of a general in chief is to keep a cool head, receiving accurate impressions from objects, and never yielding to overexcitement or being dazzled or intoxicated by the good or bad news.

****

The foremost quality of a general in chief is to have a mind that classifies the successive or simultaneous sensations it receives throughout the course of a day so that these can be seen in the proper context; for common sense and reason are the outgrowth of the comparison of several sensations taken into equal consideration.

SECRECY

(According to Napoleon, in war the first principle of a commander is to conceal what he is doing.)

See to it that no information concerning the military frontiers of the empire is published that you have not permitted and that you will deny permission for anything that could provide the enemy with useful information.

****

The minister of general police will notify all journalists that they cannot be permitted to print anything in their papers pertaining to the movements of ground and sea forces.

****

Prohibit gazettes along the border... from mentioning the army, as if it no longer exists.

****

I desire that you write the King of Spain (Joseph) to make him understand that there is nothing more contrary to military principles that to make known the strength of his army, whether in Orders of the Day and proclamations or in the gazettes.

****

The French count too much on our naivete; they would have us read like the fabled dow who leaves his prey for a mere shadow.

****

In war, the first principle of the commander is to conceal what he is doing, to see if there are ways of overcoming the obstacles, and to do everything toward this end once he has made his decision. One sees only his own problems and not those of the enemy. It is essential to display confidence.

****

You know very well (...) the importance of the most profound secrecy in such circumstances... You will employ all the demonstrations and appearances of movement that you judge convenient to deceive the enemy about the real strategical objective and persuade him that he will first be attacked by you. Therefore exaggerate your forces and announce immense and near reinforcements approaching from the interior.

Finally, you will mislead the enemy, insofar as it is possible, about the true points of attack, which are the Saint-Gotthard and the Simplon.

LEADERSHIP

(According to Napoleon, in war men are nothing; one man is everything. The presence of a commander is indispensable. Also, according to Napoleon, a commander is the head, the whole of an army. An army is nothing without the head.)

You should, by all means, encourage the soldiers to continue in the service.
This you can easily do by testifying great esteem for old soldiers.
The pay should also be increased in proportion to the years of service.
There is a great injustice in giving no higher pay to a veteran than to a recruit.

****

Nothing is more important in war than unity in command.
When, therefore, you are carrying on hostilities against a single power only, you should have but one army acting on one line and led by one commander.

****

The heart of a statesman should be in his head.

****

Instead of the lash, I would lead them by the stimulus of honor. I would instill a degree of emulation into their minds. I would promote every deserving soldier, as I did in France...

****

One obtains everything from men by appealing to their sense of honor.

****

It is exceptional and difficult to find all the qualities of a great general combined in one man.

What is most desirable and distinguishes the exceptional man, is the balance of intelligence and ability with character or courage.

If courage is predominant, the general will hazard far beyond his conceptions;

and on the contrary, he will not dare to accomplish his conceptions if his character or his courage is below his intelligence.

****

A general-in-chief should never allow any rest either to the conquerors or to the conquered.

****

Take good care of the soldier and look after him in detail. The first time that you arrive at camp, draw up the troops facing each other by battalions and inspect the soldiers, one by one, for the next eight hours. Listen to their complaints, inspect their arms, and satisfy yourself that they do not lack anything.

****

Conquerors should know the genius and the language of every religion. They ought to be Moslems in Egypt and Catholics in France, to the extent, at least, of giving sympathetic protection.

****

In the eyes of empire builders men are not men, but instruments.

****

The secret of the power to command is to be strong because in strength there is neither error nor illusion; it is truth in all its nakedness.

****

There are many advantages in making these reviews last from seven to eight hours. It accustoms the soldier to remain under arms; it demonstrates that the commander takes his responsibilities seriously and devotes himself completely to the soldier, which in turn inspires the soldier's confidence.

****

Leave them of course with the belief (...) that I will come to see them maneuver and present them with their colors.

****

What might not be expected of the English army if every soldier hoped to be made a general provided he showed the ability? (General) Bingham says, however, that most of your soldiers are brutes and must be driven by the stick. But surely the English soldiers must be possessed of sentiments sufficient to put them at least upon a level with the soldiers of other countries, where the degrading system of the lash is not used. Whatever debases man cannot be serviceable.

****

A good general, a good officer, commissioned and non-commissioned, good organization, good instruction and strict discipline make good troops independently of the cause for which they are fighting.

But enthusiasm, love of country and the desire of contributing to the national glory may also animate young troops with advantage.

Another translation:
A good general, good cadres, good organization, good instruction, and good discipline can produce good troops, regardless of the cause they fight for. It is true, however, that fanaticism, love of country, and national glory can better inspire young soldiers.

****

I value the bravery, fidelity, and loyalty of the Swiss, and this feeling has induced me to decide that all Swiss regiments should consist of Swiss citizens without any mixture of deserters or other foreigners.

****

Simply gathering men together does not produce soldiers: drill instruction and skill are what makes real soldiers. But soldiers and units amount to nothing if they are not well drilled. Make them perform maneuvers; have them take target practice; look after their health.

****

I cannot repeat it too often: act with prudence, do not compromise poor troops, and never be so foolish as to believe, like so many people, that one man automatically equates to one soldier. Troops of this nature among your soldiers require the most redoubts, earthworks, and artillery.

****

What I love about Alexander (...) is not the campaigns themselves (...) but his political means. He left behind, at age thirty-three, amongst themselves. He had the art of making conquered people love him.

****

In war men are nothing; one man is everything. The presence of the general is indispensable. He is the head, the whole of an army.

****

It was not the Roman army that subdued Gaul, but Caesar; not the Carthaginian army that caused the republic to tremble at the gates of Rome, but Hannibal; not the Macedonian army that reached the Indus, but Alexander; not the French army that carried the war to the Weser and the Inn, but Turenne; and not the Prussian army that defended Prussia for seven years against the three greatest powers of Europe, but Frederick the Great...

****

In war, only the commander understands the importance of certain things, and he alone, through his will and superior insight, conquers and surmounts all difficulties.

****

An army is nothing without the head.

****

The government must place entire confidence in its general, allow him great latitude and put forward only the objective he is to fulfill.

****

A commander is not protected by an order from a minister or a prince who is absent from the theater of operations and has little or no knowledge of the most recent turn of events.

****

Every commander responsible for executing a plan that he considers bad or disastrous is criminal: he must point out the flaws, insist that it be changed, and at last resort resign rather than be the instrument of the destruction of his own men.

****

The military institutions of the English are faulty. They recruit only for money, although they often empty their prisons into their regiments. Their discipline is cruel.
With trifling considerations, small vanities, and petty passions, it is never possible to accomplish anything great.

****

Whatever debases man cannot be serviceable.

****

Unity of command is of the first necessity in war. You must keep the army united, concentrate as many of your troops as possible on the battlefield, and take advantage of every opportunity, for fortune is a woman: if you miss her today, do not expect to find her tomorrow.

****

Every commander in chief who, as a result of superior orders, delivers a battle convinced that he will lose it, is likewise criminal.

****

I waged the campaign without consulting anyone. I could not have done it well had I been forced to reconcile my point of view with that of another.

****

I won advantages over far superior forces and with a pressing shortage of everything because convinced that I had your confidence, my march was as quick as my thoughts...

****

If you weaken your means by dividing your forces, or break the unity of military thought in Italy... you will have lost the most favorable occasion for imposing laws on Italy.

****

One always has enough troops when he knows how to use them and when the generals do not sleep in the towns but instead bivouac with their troops.

****

The Emperor cannot give you positive orders, but only general instructions because the distance is already considerable and will become greater still.

****

The conduct of generals is more delicate after battles than before because then, having been able to pursue only one course, they find themselves criticized by everybody who favored other alternatives.

****

As for me, I apply myself to follow the spirit of the instruction of the government and if by the swiftness of events, the force of circumstances and the distance involved, I have taken something on myself, this has only been with the greatest repugnance... In military operations I consult nobody; in diplomatic operations, I consult everybody.

****

In an army corps, the eye of the commander must remedy everything.

****

Captains and officers, whatever their merits might be in other respects, are constantly in a state of carelessness if the presence of the commander does not continually make itself felt.

****

Your great task is to keep all your forces together and to reach Naples as quickly as possible with your entire command... Never hold a council of war, but listen to the views of each in private... Prince Eugene, who commands in the Kingdom of Italy, will hold a reserve ready to meet any unexpected event.

****

I repeat: do not divide your forces. Let your entire army pass the Apennines and your three corps march against Naples, positioned in such a way that they can be united on the same battlefield in a single day.

****

An entire conquered people find it necessary to revolt, and I should regard a revolt (...) in the same way as the father of a family looks upon smallpox in his children: provided it does not excessively weaken the inflicted, it is a beneficial crisis.

****

A general's principal talent consists in knowing the mentality of the soldier and in winning his confidence.

****

The soldier's health must come before economy or any other consideration.

****

I give myself only half the credit for the battles I have won, and a general gets enough credit

117

when he is named at all for the fact is that a battle is won by the army.

****

A military leader must possess as much character as intellect (esprit). Men who have a great deal of intellect and little character are the least suited; they are like a ship whose masts are out of proportion to the ballast; it is preferable to have much character and little intellect.

****

Those men whose intellect is mediocre and whose character is in proportion are likely to succeed in their profession. The base must equal the height.

****

Generals who possessed intellect and character to an equally high degree were Caesar, Hannibal, Turenne, Prince Eugene (of Savoy), and Frederick (the Great).
(By character Napoleon probably means physical courage, perseverance, daring, and similar qualities. One of his favorite concepts was "squareness" which means the equilibrium of intellect and character.)

****

A general in chief is the top officer in the chain of command. The minister or prince gives instructions to which he must adhere – both in spirit and in conscience – but these instructions are never military orders and do not require passive obedience.

****

Even a direct military order requires only passive obedience when it is given by a superior who, being present at the time he gives it, knows the condition of affairs and can listen to the objections and provide explanations to those who must execute the order.

****

Well, that happens every day. It does not in itself constitute an act of disobedience. Had the prince sent him a positive order (...) it would have been obeyed... The Duke d'Orleans was recognized as commander in chief by the generals, officers, and men. None refused – or could have refused – to obey him. He is responsible for all that was done.

****

General Jourdan states in his Memoires that the government had pressured him into fighting the battle of Stockach and he seeks thus to justify himself for the unfortunate consequences of this affair. But this justification could not be allowed even when he had received a positive and formal order, as we have demonstrated. When he decided to deliver battle, he believed that he had favorable chances to win it. He deceived himself.

****

But, might it not happen that a minister or prince should explain his intentions so clearly that no clause could be misunderstood and that he says to a commander: "Deliver battle; the enemy, by virtue of his numbers, the quality of his troops, and the position that he occupies will defeat you. No matter – this is my will."

Should such an order be passively executed? No! If the general understands the benefit and consequently the morality of so strange an order, he must execute it. If he does not understand it, however, he should not obey.

****

Something of this sort often occurs in war. A battalion is left in a difficult position to save the army, but the battalion commander receives the positive order from his superior, who is present at the time he gives it and responds to all objections if there are reasonable ones to make. It is a military order given by a commander who is present and to whom one owes passive obedience. But what happens if the minister or prince is with the army? Then he takes over command, he is the commander in chief. The previous commander is no more than a subordinate division commander.

****

It does not follow that a commander in chief must not obey a minister who orders him to give battle. On the contrary, he must do it every time that, in his judgment, the judgment, the chances, and probabilities are as much for as against him, for our observation only applies in the case where the chances appear to be entirely against him.

****

The conduct of the Duke d'Orleans before Turin in 1706 has been justified: historians

121

have cleared him of all blame. The Duke d'Orleans was a prince, he had been regent, and he was of an easygoing disposition. The writers have treated him favorably, while Marchin, resting dead on the battlefield, could not defend himself. We know, however, that as he lay dying he protested the decision to remain in the lines.

But who was the commander of the French army in Italy? The Duke d'Orleans, Marchin, la Feuillade, and Albergotti were all under his orders. It was up to him whether or not he would take the advice of a council of war; he was in the chair. It was his decision whether or not to conform to the opinion of the war council. The prince did not have trouble in his command. Nobody refused to obey him. Had he given the order for the army to leave its lines, if he could give the order to the left to cross the Dora to reinforce the right; if he could have given the positive order to Albergotti to recross the Po, and the generals had refused to obey under the pretext that they did not owe him obedience, then all would be well and good. The prince would be exonerated. But, it is argued, Albergotti did not obey the order that he received to send a detachment to the right bank of the Po. He settled for making observations.

SELECTED BIBLIOGRAPHY

D'Aguilar C.B., Lieut.-Gen. Sir. G.C., *Napoleon's Military Maxims*, Translated from the French by Lieut.-Gen. Sir. G.C. D'Aguilar, C.B., Richmond VA., West & Johnston, 1862

R.M. Johnson, *The Corsican – A Diary of Napoleon's Life in His Own Words*, Boston, Houghton Mifflin Company, 1910

Hall, Henry Foljambe, *Napoleon's Letters to Josephine*, E.P. Dutton & Co., New York, 1901

Omeara, Barry Edward, *Napoleon at St. Helena*, Two volumes, Scribner and Welford, New York, New York, 1889

Bonaparte, Napoleon, Bonaparte, Joseph, *The Confidential Correspondence of Napoleon Bonaparte*, W. Clowes and Sons, London

Montholon, General Count, *History of the Captivity of Napoleon at St. Helena*, Vol I-II, Henry Colburn, London, 1846

Forsyth, William, *History of the Captivity of Napoleon at St. Helena*, Vol I-II, John Murray, London, 1853

Bertaut, Jules, *Napoleon in His Own Words*, A.C. McClurg & Co., Chicago, 1910

Luvaas, Jay, *Napoleon on the Art of War*, The Free Press, New York, 1999

Herold, J. Christopher, *The Mind of Napoleon*, Columbia University Press, New York, 1961

ABOUT THE AUTHOR

Mete Aksoy has been studying the art of war and leadership for almost twenty years. Aksoy is a graduate of Mechanical Engineering and holds a master's degree in leadership at the University of San Diego (USD). He has also received courses on negotiation and leadership at Harvard University and at M.I.T. For eighteen years, Aksoy has deepened his experience in multinational corporations in many countries of the world and is now a management consultant for various companies.

Made in the USA
Coppell, TX
01 February 2020

15224196R00074